Breaking Free From Pain

From Struggle To Strength: My Own Personal Journey With Fibromyalgia and Healing Modalities

Shari Emami, H.H.P.

Dedication

This book is dedicated to two extraordinary souls who have touched my life in profound ways, my beloved mother and Mikey. They have been a constant source of love, support, and inspiration throughout my journey, and their impact on my life is immeasurable.

Table of Contents

How to Use this Book 3

Introduction 5

Chapter 1: The Diagnosis - What is Fibromyalgia? 7

Chapter 2: Exploring the Link Between Fibromyalgia Symptoms and Hair Health **20**

Chapter 3: The Emotional Roots of Fibromyalgia: Understanding the Link Between Trauma and Chronic Pain **30**

Chapter 4: Managing Fibromyalgia in the Workplace: Strategies for Improving Working Conditions **38**

Chapter 5: Navigating the Emotional Rollercoaster of Fibromyalgia Diagnosis: Coping Strategies and Supportive Solutions **46**

Chapter 6: The Crucial Role of Your Support Network for Managing Fibromyalgia **55**

Chapter 7: Maximizing Collaborative Care: Strategies for Effective Partnership with Your Doctor and Specialists **61**

Chapter 8: Navigating the Road to Fibromyalgia Recovery: Tips for a Smoother Journey **67**

Chapter 9: How a Plant-based Diet Can Heal Fibromyalgia **83**

How To Use This Book

Welcome! I'm so glad you decided to read my book. I know that you will learn so much to take with you towards your recovery. It's going to be a great read filled with a lot of useful information that is different from what you've normally heard. In this book, I'll be sharing with you my own personal experience and healing journey with fibromyalgia. It's been a tough road, but I want you to understand that there is hope and light at the end of the tunnel. You've come this far, and I know this book will change your outlook on fibromyalgia for the better.

Please do not use this book in place of your doctor's care. Instead, use the information to expand on options that you may not be aware of. Fibromyalgia is a tricky condition, but with the right information, you can recover.

In each chapter, I will go into the potential causes of fibromyalgia and the reasons that you may have it. I'll also go into various treatment options, which ones have helped ease my pain, and how you can explore the best healing opportunities out there for you. The goal is to experiment until you find the right one. From fibromyalgia muscle workouts to alternative medicine and mineral testing, I'll go deep into how you can ease the symptoms of your disease and how to reach out to others during your path to recovery.

Ultimately, take your time reading this book. It's here to inspire and help you during your healing journey.

Introduction

Every day millions of Americans, and those who are primarily women, wake up with zero energy, as if they never got a full night's sleep. It is pure hell. This feeling is not only disabling and uncomfortable, but terrifying when it negatively impacts other areas of your life. It's hard enough to get through daily tasks while being healthy, such as family obligations, work, and self-care. With fibromyalgia, everyday life is harder as you feel so exhausted that it's hard for your body to function well and care for others.

Living with chronic pain can bring a whole set of other challenges. You're often left wondering: *Why do I feel this way*? *What is going on?*? Well, the pain I am referring to is living with fibromyalgia, as it is one aching condition that makes it hard to participate in life. It is also so often missed when it comes to a diagnosis.

Now, you're probably wondering, who am I? Well, my name is Shari Emami, I am a former fibromyalgia patient and board-certified holistic health practitioner, H.H.P. I've lived through and dealt with fibromyalgia, depression, and anxiety for years. My mission is to offer you helpful insight by sharing my point of view. I know first-hand how awful this condition is and how disabling it can be. However, there is good news. I am opening up about my personal struggle and experience in the hopes of aiding you in managing this condition with optimal care and support.

What you will get out of reading this book is a chock-full of information on methods, tests, and solutions that can provide relief. You will learn about my journey and what caused me to get to this place of finally healing as a whole person. I'm not here to make any medical claims. Instead, I am giving you my honest input on what helped me, and researched information on what helps to heal fibromyalgia. I am proud to say that I have been pain-free since 2016. I have no symptoms and I have tons of energy now. By the time you finish reading this book, my hope is that you will reach this place of healing as well. After all, I'm living proof that there is hope. Here is my story.

Chapter One

The Diagnosis -What is Fibromyalgia?

It's 2014 on a hot September day and I am sitting in the patient's chair wondering what my doctor is about to tell me. I've been frustrated for months now because of my seemingly never-ending pain and frustrating lack of answers. It was like a combination of a burning, stabbing, and prickly feeling inside my muscles and all throughout my body. But, at this point, I had already been to an internal medicine doctor who had failed to diagnose me. I wasn't sure what to do, so here I was in the office not knowing that the news that was broken to me would change my life.

"How long have you had these muscle aches before?" she asked. I replied and said, "Not too long, only about five months." Then, she asked me where the pain was and I pointed to each part of my body that was hurting. This included the back of the neck, the knee area, hip area, ankle, behind the calf, shoulder, and forearm. When I was finally done guiding her through all of my areas of pain, she paused and entered a deep train of thought. Then she lowered her voice. She looked at my medical chart and just sighed.

"Well, there are about 18 pressure points on this, but I believe you have fibromyalgia." According to my doctor, the 18 pressure points reside in these areas:

-Knee

-Edge of upper breast

-Arm near the elbow

-Lower neck region

-Base of the skull in the back of the head

-Hip bone

-Upper outer buttock

-Back of the neck

-Back of the shoulders

My mouth dropped in disbelief. I know my mother had fibromyalgia when I was little, but it went away. When she had fibromyalgia, she was in chronic pain and was taking care of both me and my brother. From what she described, it was aching tiredness all over. This can't be happening right now I thought to myself.

I shrieked, "My mom had it! It went away after a year." The doctor turned and looked at me right in the eye. "Well, what she had wasn't fibromyalgia. Usually, in these cases, it's lifelong. The pain just doesn't go away on its own either. I can give you medicine, though, and see if that helps."

I was already diagnosed with depression and anxiety, and now this incurable, lifelong disorder called fibromyalgia. I was crushed and my spirit was shattered. Then and there, I broke down in tears right in front of the doctor.

The first question that popped into my head was, *Am I going to be able to work? Will I be in pain at work?* After all, I just got my board certification that month as a holistic health practitioner. I asked my doctor what the future looked like for me. She said that a lot of people just find ways to cope with pain and if I want to ever apply for SSDI or SSI, (social security disability insurance), and the (supplemental security income) program, that could be an option too. However, I did not want to apply for disability mainly for my own pride and career goals. I also would feel stripped away from any dignity and looked down upon by my family members.

I couldn't believe my ears. Nothing made sense to me and I could not figure out why now, out of all times, to get this diagnosis. Just did not make sense to me.

She explained to me the different medicines that were available and treatment options. My head felt like it was spinning. I was already on antidepressants and anxiety meds for PTSD (post-traumatic stress disorder) and anxiety. I did not know if adding more medication would be a wise decision. However, I was desperate to try something because it was very painful. My doctor also looked like she had no idea what to say to me.

I walked out of the doctor's office still in tears, but no one saw me cry. I went home and started researching fibromyalgia, what causes it, and everything else I could find out about the condition that was now a part of my identity.

A week ago, prior to this visit, I went to see a massage therapist and got a deep tissue massage. During the massage, she said she never felt the muscles doing that before. I was puzzled and asked her to elaborate more and explain it to me. She said that they felt like they were popping, almost like the visual of popcorn being made. She went deeper into the muscles, but she could not find any specific sore spots or source of the pain. She said she's never worked with anyone where the muscles felt like that. I did not know what to do so I made an appointment with my general practitioner. I figured maybe I also needed to see a rheumatologist.

Alright, now what exactly is fibromyalgia? Well, the name is actually derived from the Latin "fibro," meaning fibrous tissues; "my," meaning muscles and "algia," meaning pain. It is known to affect about 4 million Americans, about 2 percent of the population. It's more common among women than men. However, it can affect people of all ages, including children and men. Some men have reported milder symptoms including irritable bowel syndrome and fatigue. However, it is most commonly diagnosed among women ages 20 to 50. The majority of people are diagnosed during middle age and you are more likely to have fibromyalgia as you get older. I got diagnosed at the age of 34. It is known as a lifelong disorder with no cure.

Debunking the Myths:

However, what I discovered is that it's not all black or white. Here are 10 myths about fibromyalgia. These myths are all entirely false.

1. It's not a real disorder- this is not true.
2. All the pain is made up and all in your head.
3. You're faking your tiredness.
4. You will never recover.
5. Exercise will make things worse.
6. Alternative medical treatments are a waste of time and money providing no benefits.
7. This only affects women.

8. You'll never be able to work again.
9. It's a form of arthritis.
10. It's just an autoimmune disorder.

Prior to what you've heard before, and according to doctors, fibromyalgia isn't an autoimmune disorder, but one that deals with the way the brain responds to pain. Unlike other joint disorders, there is no disfiguring like you would see in perhaps rheumatoid arthritis. You look completely fine and healthy and no one can tell that you're sick, which is one of the reasons it can be so hard to get a correct diagnosis.

To put it simply, fibromyalgia is a disorder that involves widespread musculoskeletal pain along with fatigue, sleep, memory, and mood issues. Sounds fun right? Researchers believe that fibromyalgia amplifies painful sensations by affecting the way your brain and spinal cord process painful and non-painful signals. It sort of tricks the muscles into thinking they are sore when they really aren't; it's just your brain's way of processing the brain improperly.

Currently, it is said that there is no single cause of fibromyalgia and it's chronic and lifelong. I personally feel that it's caused by both emotional and physical issues in the body. A lot of doctors misdiagnose this condition and sometimes write it off as a mental illness. Trust me, it's not all in your head. There is a physical component to it and even certain gene expressions can make you susceptible to developing fibromyalgia.

Prior to being diagnosed, I was experiencing symptoms that my primary care physician could not pick up on. Frustrated, I took the liberty and purchased my own blood work from a third party, and got tested at Quest diagnostics. I looked for the TSH (thyroid stimulating hormone) levels for the thyroid and the T3 and T4 (triiodothyronine), and (thyroxine) to get a better picture. A lot of times doctors will just rule out thyroid issues by basing their assumption on the TSH levels. However, it doesn't always give the full picture, which is why further tests need to be ordered. I also ordered the thyroid antibodies test and ANA, (anti-nuclear antibodies) as it could explain why I was feeling so tired. The ANA test looks for any antibodies or viruses in the system that are attacking healthy cells. It's a good indicator if there is an autoimmune illness in the system. It's a good idea to go further in the system and check at a cellular level to see what could be going on. I'll get more into that later in chapter two.

I felt confused, frustrated, and afraid as I had to research and speculate what to look for. Since inflammation was my main target, I tested for the SED also known as erythrocyte sedimentation rate (ESR). It can reveal inflammatory activity in the body. I also did another inflammatory marker test called CK (creatine kinase) which can detect if there is muscle damage. I thought maybe I tore something and that's why I was in pain. Sometimes, if you have tingling or muscle aches, which I did, this can be an important test. High results can indicate adrenal issues or muscle damage as well. I also thought about the ELISA (enzyme-linked immunoassay) blood test for Lyme disease just in case, even though I had no exposure to ticks. Sometimes symptoms of fibromyalgia mimic Lyme disease. I passed on it due to the price.

I also did a full women's profile which checked my metabolic rate and full system to look at kidney and liver function. I ordered an estrogen and progesterone blood panel all of which I paid for myself. I must have spent close to $1,000 on all the tests. None of my doctors would run these tests even if I asked for them. It's no wonder that people often think fibromyalgia is all in their head.

The only thing that can back a bit off was low thyroid but not enough to diagnose as Hashimoto's or hypothyroidism. I just started to take supplements for the thyroid, which I would advise you to be careful of.

So, why is fibromyalgia so often misdiagnosed? One of the reasons is because up until recently, it was not considered a legitimate medical condition. Another reason is that it does not show up on x-rays or blood work. It also overlaps with other conditions so it can be tricky to get a proper diagnosis. Doctors can only go based on the patient's symptoms. They then can create a possible diagnosis through that. This sometimes creates confusion for a proper diagnosis. My doctor was very smart, though, and right on point for recognizing it.

As I was searching the internet for anything I could find out about my new disease after I had been diagnosed, I found two likely causes. Both psychological and physical. I looked back at my life and I did experience great emotional distress. It led to PTSD and physical trauma. I did get out of several emotionally abusive relationships with men, survived the assault, and I did get in a brutal car accident in 2008. I remember it like it was yesterday. Driving on the freeway going to a job interview. The tire got a flat and the car swung around and did a 360 while I pulled myself out of the car. The car got smashed into a wall and there I was in the middle of the freeway with road rash, a second degree burn and blood coming down my nose. I was immediately taken to the hospital. Luckily, all my bumps and bruises healed, no scars, no injury, but emotionally, I felt damaged. My body was sore, however, for about six months afterwards. The doctors performed a head scan, but nothing came back on my MRI, as everything was fine.

Mentally, it was rough trying to put my life back together and feel less traumatized. I started showing symptoms of PTSD and would get recurring dreams about the crash for the next six months. To this day, I still do not like driving on the freeway. It was one of the reasons I was on antidepressants as well as past relationship experiences that led me to feeling down all the time. Then this, just as I was slowly starting to heal, the diagnosis happens. That wasn't the worst of it.

Nothing could explain the bizarre physical symptoms I was experiencing. This included the fibro fog, concentration issues, digestive problems and pins and needles in my legs. I have to say that fibro fog is the worst, as it feels like an extreme case of brain fog. It literally feels like there are cotton balls in your head. It is utterly impossible to function or concentrate with this symptom. It makes it hard to function and perform everyday tasks.

Another issue was my period. When my menstruation would arrive, my cramps felt worse than ever. It felt like a knife slicing my uterus. It was brutal. Traditional pain relievers only did so much to alleviate my pain.

One time, the strangest thing happened. I remembered my right lower leg swelled up and I thought it was a blood clot. I went to the emergency room and the nurse told me that it was nothing, merely that fibromyalgia is an emotional problem, and told me to do low-impact workouts. She then asked me why I was so anxious. I explained to her that I was a bit nervous about my leg. She kindly listened but dismissed my concerns.

As I was looking at boards on the internet, I discovered that other fibromyalgia patients have experienced similar symptoms to mine. Either their legs or ankles would swell for a while and then go down.

There were other times where all I could do was lie in bed hopeless about my future. At my lowest point, I was so depressed and had suicidal thoughts. When you're in that much pain, you think of the worst things possible. It was 24/7 burning in my body. If there was a drawing of fibromyalgia, it would be a body on fire.

Let's not forget about the head pain. The headaches were unbearable beyond belief. I'm talking about shooting stabbing ice pick headaches. Sometimes, it was a fuzzy feeling in the head and bad temporal headaches. It felt like my brain was on fire. Seriously, you would think I had a tumor or mass growing in there. However, it was all symptoms of fibromyalgia, as they call it, fibro fog.

The digestive issues were another story and they were hard to deal with as well. A lot of cramping and spastic colon issues. It was awful.

Getting out of bed was hard for me and walking was awkward because a lot of pain would reside in my foot and on top of the extensor tendons, which is the top of my foot. Sometimes it was too hard to walk and I would just stay in bed crying.

I was just so frustrated and I did not know what to do. I tried quite a number of things, including acupuncture, massages, and even though these helped temporarily, the symptoms would reappear after four or five months. I did try medication for fibromyalgia, but it gave me weird dreams at night and did not help me feel better at all. I also tried taking cayenne pepper supplements because they helped a bit with the pain. However, after using them every day, I developed stomach cramping and bloating. Everything I had tried only provided temporary relief or horrible side effects that made it not worth trying at all. This was not looking too bright for me.

I wasn't working at the time, but a typical day would go like this for me: Wake up and lie in bed for ten minutes, try to muster all my strength to get out of bed and then start meditating. I would then try to cook an anti-inflammatory meal such as eggs, avocados and toast, or sometimes just whole wheat cereal with fruit. The thought of trying to get some movement in was daunting, so I just focused on light movements by working my arms and body. Then, I would read and try to look for a job.

Then, one day, there was a new discovery. I met a naturopath in 2015 who ran a urine test instead of a blood test. He wanted to get my metabolites and a reading on my system and hormones. He actually found a gene expression called MTHFR in my urine. It stands for methylenetetrahydrofolate reductase, which is a mutation that heightens homocysteine in the system. I was also depleted of folic acid which could be corrected with supplements. A lack of folic acid also causes higher homocysteine levels. The naturopath stated that the gene mutation could be the underlying cause of fibromyalgia. There is truth to it, and studies have shown with scientific research that MTHFR makes a person more susceptible to fibromyalgia. The trick to this is to lower homocysteine levels, this can be done by working out, an anti-inflammatory diet, and good amounts of folic acid.

Another interesting finding was that my hormones were off

balance and my cortisol levels were through the roof. Cortisol gets released when the body is under stress. The naturopath laughed at me and wondered how I got out of bed in the morning. I felt so humiliated. I invested all this time into my health and now this. As a patient, especially with fibromyalgia, it's important to find a doctor that will listen to you. Please don't ever work with a doctor that makes you feel unheard or bad about yourself. I went to get a second opinion and yes I had the gene, but there were things I could do to help lower cortisol levels and damper homocysteine levels. Some of which include simple vitamin therapy, diet, and exercise. At first, nothing worked. Later on in Chapter 9, I will explain how the right diet helped me with my symptoms.

By this point, I was living a nightmare. There were days where I felt like I could not take the muscle aches and burning any longer. The worst part is that people tell you that you don't look sick. However, past the surface, the body feels like all the tender points are on fire. All this interest in studying holistic health and my own health was suffering. The worst part was that I had to turn down invites to places because I was just too unbelievably tired to go. Some of my friends thought I was lazy or making an excuse. I explained to them how I was feeling and eventually they got it, but the invites as a result got less and less, and it didn't help that on the outside I looked completely fine. Nobody seemed to validate or see my pain.

However, I wanted to remain hopeful and was ready to get back to working, but I wanted to see if my naturopath could treat me. He suggested the paleo diet and ketogenic diet, but after a while, I did not feel comfortable eating that much protein vs carbs. He suggested I read a book about how wheat sensitivity causes and makes fibromyalgia worse. He wanted me to try elimination diets to see if that would help. It was okay, but never provided me full relief.

In addition to this, I slowly eased myself back into a light workout routine. It was different from the usual circuit training that I was used to. Another suggestion was water aerobics, but I did not have access to a pool. What I did instead was stick with a light jog and fast walking routine in the morning. Then for strength, I used a resistance band. No weights. The naturopath suggested heavy weights and that was too painful for me. No thank you.

I was hoping that eventually after doing the light workouts that I could build up to the usual HIIT training and running, but I couldn't for some time. I did, however, do cycling and brisk walking. Anything helped to ease the pain and keep the joints limber and feeling better.

It took a while to assimilate into the right diet. Often, for those with fibromyalgia, we all have unique experiences, so finding a diet that works for you will likely be a time of trial and error. Personally, I was not really into the ketogenic diet as I found it was hard to maintain. All those eggs, cheeses and meats made my digestion worse. The paleo diet was not any better. The only two diets that worked and helped me out for fibromyalgia were the Mediterranean diet and plant-based diet. I'm more partial to vegan and pescatarian diets because it's very anti-inflammatory and I love animals. A lot of illnesses' root causes are caused by inflammation. I will discuss more about my decision to go plant-based later in chapter 9. The benefits are also backed by NASM (National Academy of Sports Medicine), resources and even include a great shopping guide for you to follow.

There is an upside. With proper care and making it a daily habit to stay on top of treatment, I'm living proof that you can recover from this brutally painful condition. It takes a lot of trial and error, but I know you can do it. You owe it to yourself to take care of your body and allow it to heal properly. I have been completely pain-free since 2016, and I want the same for you.

Chapter Two

Exploring the Link Between Fibromyalgia Symptoms and Hair Health

When I became board certified as a holistic health practitioner back in 2014, one of the healing modalities I offered was hair mineral analysis. I would not use this in place of blood work for checking for deficiencies. However, if nothing comes back in the blood work and you're still feeling a bit off, I would highly recommend this testing. The hair testing often picks up changes in minerals and heavy metals in the body that haven't been picked up by the blood. This test can even go further into the body and detect deficiencies that blood work might not have picked up, especially if you're still experiencing any symptoms that could relate to fibromyalgia. One of the things that hair mineral testing can pick up that blood can't, is the ability to detect mineral imbalances and toxicity in the system. An imbalance could cause all types of problems and inflammation in the body resulting in fibromyalgia symptoms.

The lab I used for this testing was Analytical Research Labs in Arizona. The founding father of this testing was the late Dr. Paul C. Eck, who was a brilliant biochemist, clinician, and physician who specialized in mineral balancing. He spent most of his life researching psychology, nutrition and biochemistry. He founded the hair mineral analysis testing as a way to look at mineral deficiencies to re-balance the system with nutrition. Dr. Eck realized that the HTMA (hair testing mineral analysis) was actually measuring the body's response to stress rather than simply looking at the separate mineral levels on a hair test. All the mineral levels had to be interpreted as a whole to look at the body's entire system. Dr. Eck's theories and ideas were cutting-edge, in the manner that he used all these concepts to help understand the significance of tissue mineral levels, ratios and metabolic patterns. He used this information to look at the causes of many types of diseases. As a result, he became the main authority figure in hair mineral testing and technically the first person to discover this type of testing method. Dr. Eck found his findings effective and fascinating. In 1974, he opened up Analytical Research labs and it has been open ever since.

I used it in the past for patients who had a wide variety of issues including thyroid imbalances, hormonal problems and mineral deficiencies. Some of my patients would call me for a test to help their child with ADHD (attention deficit hyperactivity disorder), and other issues. In the past, after finding patients' results and receiving nutritional therapy, they have reported feeling better overall, likely because it helped them get to the root of the problem. It's a great test to participate in.

Even though I no longer offer this testing, I would highly advise considering it if you have fibromyalgia or persistent symptoms. An HMTA or hair mineral testing can show signs of mineral deficiencies that can give a clearer picture of what could be causing symptoms, thus knowing how to naturally treat it. You can go to any doctor or any holistic practitioner to order it. Be careful of hair mineral testing that you can purchase online.

They just provide the test, but no interpretations. There has been a lot of controversy over HTMA in the past, but what people don't realize is that even though it's not a medical test, only an alternative medicine test, it still provides great value. One of the points made was that it was unreliable, however it has been shown that hair testing can provide crucial and useful information about someone's metabolic rate, energy levels, carbohydrate tolerance, stage of stress, immune system, and glandular activity. A lot of issues with problems at the cellular level, can predict further problems that could happen as an outcome. It is important to remember that rebalancing the system is one key ingredient to feeling healthier overall.

I advise you to follow up with a holistic doctor after testing. Please don't use hair testing as a replacement for blood testing though given by your primary doctor, only use it as an add-on test to see what else could be going on. It's well worth the cost.

So, what exactly *is* a hair mineral analysis? A hair mineral analysis or HTMA is an alternative medicine form of non-invasive testing that looks at the hair to test and give a blueprint of what's going on in the system. It can show cellular activity within the body. It goes as far back as 3-4 months of metabolic testing to look for mineral deficiencies. A hair analysis uses special techniques to closely look at the hair. What is interesting is that the results can show details about your health and habits.

Here's the reason why it's a great form of testing. First off, there are no needles or drawing blood as it's non-invasive. The reason why it's effective is that your hair absorbs chemicals from the medications you take, the foods you eat, and environmental toxins, and this information stays in the hair shaft for several months. It can test for thyroid issues, mineral deficiencies, toxicities in the system and nutritional imbalances.

To do this type of testing, you purchase the test from a holistic practitioner and at home and either you or a friend snips your clean hair close to the scalp. The hair should be dry. It's also best to work on chemically untreated hair to get the most accurate results. That means no dye, perms, Brazilian blowouts, etc. What I recommend is, if it is treated, to wait about 6-8 weeks till the hair grows back and then use the new hair for testing. The sample of the hair is then put in an envelope and mailed to the lab. Usually, the test will offer a symptoms list that you can check off as well. The ends of the hair, which is over three millimeters long, are cut off and thrown away. The testing laboratory requires about a tablespoon of hair. Then, laboratory technicians cut the sample into small pieces and dissolve it in acid overnight. The measured portion amount is then burned in a computer-controlled spectrometer. Each mineral gives off specific L kilo colors or spectra, which are read by sensitive detectors. The test is actually divided into three parts: macro minerals, trace minerals, and toxic metals. The test gives a value to each element.

The macro minerals include calcium, magnesium, sodium, and potassium. The trace minerals include zinc, copper, selenium, iron, chromium, manganese, cobalt, boron, and molybdenum. The last are the toxic metals which in high amounts lead to poisoning. These include arsenic, cadmium, lead, aluminum, and mercury. As you can see, heavy amounts of toxic metals can be deadly.

Now, how is this all related to fibromyalgia? Well, it can be seen in a number of ways with this type of testing. According to Analytical Research Labs, the root cause of many pain disorders is adrenal blow out or insufficiency. Most people with the diagnosis of fibromyalgia are slow oxidizers. Slow oxidizers mean that food converts into energy at a slower rate. This means that the metabolism is slower and their adrenal glands are underactive. When your adrenal glands are under active you typically feel tired, lethargic and have no energy.

High Calcium Levels and Muscular Pain

One thing that came back on my hair test was high calcium. When hair calcium levels are very high, it is a marker for fibromyalgia. What was clear was that my hair testing results showed that hair calcium levels were higher and magnesium levels were significantly lower than healthy individuals' test results. High levels of calcium also dictate that it is not being properly absorbed. This creates a problem in the way the muscles feel and respond to pain. It is not clearly shown why, but another thing that can happen is that high calcium can cause a condition known as hyperparathyroidism. This is when your body produces too much of the parathyroid hormone. The parathyroid hormone produced by the thyroid glands helps maintain the right balance of calcium in the bloodstream and in tissue. The right amount of calcium is essential for proper functioning. This is especially important for nerve and muscle function, as well as bone health. When the calcium is too high, it affects muscle pain.

What is interesting is that hyperparathyroidism can mimic symptoms of fibromyalgia. It's not definite what percentage of people with high calcium can get this condition, and it's not exactly clear what percentage of patients with high calcium lead to fibromyalgia. However, it still is an important topic and to not be ignored because there are so many ways calcium affects the muscles and function. Therefore, an imbalance could cause discomfort and pain.

Low Magnesium and Fibromyalgia Symptoms

Another thing that is common with fibromyalgia patients is extremely low magnesium. Magnesium deficiency is usually related to a lot of leg and muscle cramping. This would explain the correlation between low magnesium and fibromyalgia symptoms. Most people don't get enough magnesium in their diet and they must consume it through sources that include nuts, low fat dairy and leafy greens. Taking magnesium supplements personally helped me deal with fibromyalgia pain as it relaxes the muscles and helps with leg cramping.

Low Sodium and Potassium Levels in Fibromyalgia Patients

Another finding in fibromyalgia patients is when their sodium and potassium levels are low. The imbalance of the sodium/potassium ratio is often present in the hair analysis of those with fibromyalgia. According to the works and findings of the late Dr. Paul Eck, the sodium/potassium ratio on a hair mineral analysis reflects the balance between the pro-inflammatory and the anti-inflammatory hormones. Any elevated pro-inflammatory response would cause inflammation and pain to elevate in the body. There are certain anti-inflammatory foods you can eat that will help calm down inflammation. I will discuss some of these inflammation solutions in Chapter 9.

Copper Toxicity and Fibromyalgia

According to findings and research with Analytical Research Labs, toxic metal build up can contribute to some cases of fibromyalgia. Among the most commonly seen is copper toxicity. Copper is required for energy production in the electron transport system. About 30% of our cellular energy in the form of ATP (adenosine triphosphates) is generated here. A copper imbalance profoundly affects energy production. ATP is energy stored and used at the cellular level. An excess amount of copper would affect ATP, which would cause energy depletion that is found in fibromyalgia.

As you can see there are quite a few causes of toxic metals that can increase fibromyalgia risks. You're probably wondering what you can do to help remedy the situation with what's going on in your system. Well, it would be wise to detoxify the system and get rid of any toxins. What is a toxin exactly? Well, it's anything that does not belong in the body, whether man-made or natural. There are many ways your body is exposed to toxins. Some include environmental toxins such as metals, plastics, and radiation, to name a few. Some can even be emotional toxins from stress and negative thinking patterns. The goal is to get rid of these toxins so that the body can heal.

In the detoxification process, your whole body starts to eliminate those toxins. The main organs that expel toxins include the kidneys, large intestines, liver, lungs and skin. These are big parts of the human body, but that's not enough. In order to fully detoxify, the system has to release toxins from every cell.

That is how the body heals on a cellular level. It was actually this information that propelled Dr. Eck to researching hair testing and discovering the benefits. He also states that getting to the cell activity can be the root of a lot of ailments including fibromyalgia.

Let me explain further. Hair is a great form of biopsy as it can easily be collected and transported. It also tracks minerals in the body. As hair grows, it imprints a permanent record of the body's nutritional deficiencies. This can show what is happening on a cellular level. Having your body get healthy with each cell can be the utmost form of healing. It also allows the body to function on an optimal level. Getting the whole body and system back to balance can really be beneficial at alleviating symptoms and root causes of fibromyalgia.

In regards to healing, when the body detoxifies, it allows the cells to heal. There are many ways you can avoid toxins so that the body does not get overloaded with this. One is keeping a healthy lifestyle. That means nourishing your body, mind and spirit. The other is reducing your exposure to poisons.

Both medical and dental toxins are to be of caution such as amalgam dental fillings, or silver fillings. Another is a list of other poisons that can create toxicity in the body. Please note that if you have to be on these try to ask your dentist for a more natural option to fillings or implants such as composite resin fillings.

Prescription drugs create side effects in the body especially if used long-term, so be careful. Always listen to your doctor and see if you can reduce or make lifestyle changes to help. Anything else such as NSAIDS like aspirin, radiation from X-rays, breast implants, MRIs. Obviously, you can't avoid everything, but be mindful and understand what the side effects are. Always keep an open communication with your doctor.

Another form of toxins is in how we think. When we think bad and melancholy thoughts, we physically feel bad. Negative thoughts produce a reaction and chemical changes in the brain. This is because thoughts change the brain and being stuck in a loop of negativity will cause havoc to the limbic system. Watch your thoughts. Try to be as positive as possible and always stay mindful. Do not be stuck in the past. Keep moving forward.

Lastly, nourish your body with healthy foods. Avoid sugar, white flour, and overly processed foods. For me personally, a vegan diet with moderate carbohydrates works best at helping me heal. I just feel better overall and my pain is reduced. I talk more about how to find the right diet for you in the last chapter.

Another thing that is found to be true is that there is a strong link to slow oxidizers and developing fibromyalgia. Slow oxidizers feel best when they eat lower levels of protein and fat. Excessive protein and fat at a meal can make them feel tired and lethargic. This might be one of the reasons why a vegan diet worked best for me. I will discuss more about the benefits of a plant-based diet in Chapter 9.

Remember, always be careful with what you put in your body and who you surround yourself with. Your job is to detox and reset your system. Think of junk food and processed food, for example, as garbage. Garbage in and garbage out. The same goes for toxic thoughts. Replace those depleted minerals with the correct supplements, diet, and vitamins. Replace negative thoughts with positive ones. Your brain and body will start to feel better when you do this. Your thinking will be more clear, and you will have more energy and less pain as a result.

Chapter 3

The Emotional Roots of Fibromyalgia: Understanding the Link Between Trauma and Chronic Pain

Content Warning: This chapter explores themes around emotional and physical abuse.

In the fall of 2009, I met a man who I thought was amazing. His name was Adam. He was cute, funny, sweet, and had everything else that I'd always wanted in a partner. He was the whole package. I met him at the community YMCA in one of the adult painting classes. We hit it off immediately and I began spending a lot of time with him. Before I knew it, I was smitten. I was completely in love with this man and he said he felt the same way.

Adam and I were attached at the hip, we did everything together. We went on hikes, went camping, and had romantic movie nights. He was really into health and wellness too, which I liked. It was so much fun working out together. I spent a lot of time at his house and got to meet his parents, but something started to change when he decided to go into the air force. His decision was sudden, but I fully supported it.

He was stationed in Texas for about ten weeks. He would write to me every week explaining basic training and how grueling it was and what his day was like. After he came back home to visit, everything took a turn for the worst. He became a different and frightening person.

When he came home from Texas, he was at my door with a surprise visit and flowers in his hand. I was so happy and grateful. We got to spend time together and do our usual activities, but then his personality started to change. He went from a caring, understanding man who checked all of my boxes in a romantic partner to an emotionally and physically abusive person.

By this point, Adam really began to frighten me. He was like a loose cannon. If he didn't want to watch a TV show that was on, he would get nasty and reprimand me. He began to control what I wore and how I did my makeup. I could not have an opinion on anything from interests, current events and politics. I felt suffocated. I couldn't make plans with my friends and in the rare event that I *did* get to see them, Adam would want to know every personal detail about them. I thought that this was a bit strange.

He became increasingly aggressive towards me and I did not know how to defend myself or walk away. He would sometimes slap me, push me, or pull my hair. One time he slapped me so hard that my lip started to bleed a bit. He would call me very cruel names if I didn't do what he wanted.

In addition, his statements were quite disturbing and alarming. He would say he owned the right to sleep with me. When I was in the hospital after my car accident, he did not visit me. He was callous at times and exhibited classic symptoms of a textbook psychopath. In addition, he would put me down a lot and criticize me for the smallest of things, from what I wore to what I watched, who I hung out with, and how I spent my time.

He was mentally, emotionally and physically hurting me. I felt alone, helpless and isolated. I confided to a dear friend that I had met in college and she urged me to leave him. I did just that.

I broke up with him, but he did not let me go. As is typical with the seemingly inescapable cycle of abuse, I ended up forgiving him. But, after two months, we broke up again. I guess the cycle continued and I could not take it anymore. I completely ended it for good. However, the damage was permanent. I had to go on antidepressants and I blamed myself a lot. I felt quite a bit of shame and my self-esteem grew very low.

Afterward, I got a new job writing for a newspaper. It was super exciting but also super stressful. In fact, the stress made me so anxious that I had to see my doctor, who ended up diagnosing me with depression, anxiety, and PTSD from my abusive relationship.

The PTSD symptoms that ensued were terrible. I had horrible flashbacks and nightmares. It felt like I was walking down a dark tunnel not knowing what or who was on the other end. Often, I could still feel his presence and even smell him. I could remember how cold he was inside and how he had a dead soul. This aura would follow me in the most unpredictable places. Even when I was at the store in a non-threatening situation, it still would feel like I was trapped with him. PTSD is quite debilitating and scary, because the symptoms and memories follow you no matter where you are. For me, this included extreme panic attacks and general nervousness. If I went out with a guy, my fight or flight would be triggered and I would immediately assume that I was in danger. So, I stopped dating all together.

The aftermath of any emotional or physical trauma can

manifest itself in the body in many ways. Emotions are located in the limbic system, and trauma can activate the amygdala and stay stored in the hippocampus, which is responsible for memory. Any emotional distress can start affecting the brain and the way it responds to pain. Any disruption to these pain responses can trigger fibromyalgia to develop.

You're probably wondering: *How can this happen?* Say you've been exposed to past trauma, let's say an assault, the death of a loved one, or an accident. As a result, your stress responses get activated and the fight or flight response goes into overdrive, activating stress. This results in altering normal development and reactions to stress and painful stimuli. When the brain gets affected by this, it changes the way it responds to pain creating a widespread response to the brain. It causes a misfire in the brain causing the person to feel pain even if there is no visible injury.

As far as taking control of this, I decided to try anti-depressants. I went on quite a few meds to alleviate my symptoms. However, the side effects were awful. I would have body jerks at night and my hands would be shaking a lot. I would get brutal headaches. It was challenging trying to find the right cocktail of drugs. I say medicines are only necessary as a last resort for those with fibromyalgia, because the side effects are often so much more overwhelming than the temporary relief.

As noted in terms of other trauma, the physical impact of my car accident caused soreness in my body, but most importantly, it caused a lot of emotional distress. The truth is that any stress on the body can be a recipe for developing fibromyalgia. It plants the seeds for the condition to grow. Now, it was all starting to make sense to me.

With all that I've been through, I decided to quit my job in 2011 at the newspaper and decided to try therapy. I worked on trying to stay positive and discussed what I was feeling. I'll discuss this a bit later.

As is common with many victims of abuse, I began to blame myself for allowing him to have so much power over me. I reclaimed that power back my studying emotions and holistic healing. In 2013, I studied lifestyle management and sports injury specialist from NESTA (National Exercise and Sports Trainer Association), and took continuing education units in various ailments at Bastyr University and Cleveland Clinic. I also studied Integrative Mental Health from University of Central Florida. I obtained a few other certifications and then in 2014 I applied and got Board Certified by American Association of Drugless Practitioners as a Holistic Health Practitioner. I also studied and got certified in health coaching from the prestigious Dr. Sears Wellness Institute. This all gave me the motivation to help myself and help others work through their own trauma and heal.

When I first studied alternative medicine, I did not know what direction I wanted to go into, but I knew that I wanted to deal with treating the body as a whole. I think it's important to incorporate Western medicine with Eastern medicine philosophies for a more effective and holistic treatment plan. It's your health and you owe it to yourself to use both and see what works for you. Do not ignore or deny treatment plans that your doctor instructs, but also use other forms as well, such as acupuncture, non-invasive diagnostic testing, herbs, aromatherapy, yoga, and anything else that you think will make you feel better. Experiment around, see what is effective, and then decide what you like best.

Another key component to healing is finding a good community of support. I go to church to help me, but it doesn't have to be a church, but some kind of faith-based community where you can receive support. You need to be around loving caring people to help you get through this and get closer to healing. You need to see the bigger picture beyond yourself as this setback to grow as a person. It really does help to have people to talk to that share the same belief and common ground. It will give you comfort and peace.

To say the least, trauma is a tricky thing. It not only affects you emotionally, but physically. I'll never forget how free I felt when I broke up with Adam. It was liberating and refreshing. Unfortunately, the side effects of being with him, and the car accident caused a long bout of depression and chronic pain. Turns out, when you're in emotional distress, your body reacts to it as well. This was definitely a contributing factor to what caused my fibromyalgia. I say if you can, try to book an appointment and speak with a therapist and have them help you deal with your emotions.

What I tried that worked was a combination of meditation and mindfulness. I did DBT, which is dialectical behavior therapy. This type of therapy focuses on mindfulness and breathing and was developed by Dr. Marsha Linehan. It's great for those suffering emotionally and in chronic pain. Some of the focuses include radical acceptance, which is accepting things as they are without trying to change it. You accept the situation as is, but look at ways to instead be in the moment. It helped me a lot with my PTSD. It also allows you to look at chronic conditions in a whole new manner. In order to heal, I had to change my attitude about fibromyalgia pain. I know first-hand how heartbreaking, upsetting and brutally painful it is to suffer from chronic pain. I also understand how hard and it is to seek help for any type of emotional scars you have. You need to talk to someone and heal. It's so important and good for you. The emotions are composed in the limbic system, and when it becomes healthy you will feel better and so will your body.

It will make a profound difference to go to therapy, so book an appointment with a therapist. Make sure that you find someone you can trust and you click with. If you're not working due to fibromyalgia, you can apply for low-cost insurance and look at some therapists that are in the network. Don't let anything prevent you from seeking treatment. You are worth it. I can now say that I'm a survivor of domestic and emotional abuse.

With fibromyalgia, something like a car accident can cause stress on the muscles. As far as emotional trauma, the emotions sit in the brain never resolving, but instead start to affect the brain as well as the body. There has always been a mind-body connection in health. Your emotions play an important role and can affect everything in your system and in the way that you feel. It has been known that great levels of distress can cause fibromyalgia. I just remember it all happened one day waking up feeling my body was on fire. It was years after that I started experiencing the pain and it's still not clear if it was something such as MTHFR that triggered fibromyalgia or all the physical and emotional trauma. Perhaps it was a combination of both. It kind of fascinates me how repressed emotions and unresolved feelings can manifest itself into the physical body. We really are our mind, body and spirit. In conclusion, in order to achieve true health, all three must be properly balanced.

Chapter 4

Managing Fibromyalgia in the Workplace: Strategies for Improving Working Conditions

To work or not to work. That is a question that is going to be running through your mind a lot. The thing is, working is a personal decision but most times a necessity. We all have bills to pay and we all need ways to make ends meet. However, if you have just been recently diagnosed with fibromyalgia, you may be wondering if you'll be able to go back to your old job.

I'm here to help you find some solutions that I didn't know about when I was diagnosed. Let's discuss some viable options when it comes to maintaining good working conditions. One possible solution is to ask your boss if you can only go in half the time. If your boss says no, then feel free to explain your condition and see if both of you can come up with a solution. Another option is to see if you can telecommute or set up a hybrid situation where you only go in person some of the time. By working remotely, you'll gain time to take care of yourself and get that much needed rest.

That being said, work is important to our well-being and can give us a sense of purpose in life. When we don't work, a lot of times we can feel lost. I know for me, I always need to find purpose in something. It's been said that those that do work, report higher self-esteem and life satisfaction. The trick is to find the right job that can accommodate your needs with fibromyalgia. There are some specific things to make note of when job searching, and I will mention that to you in a bit.

Some things to aim for are jobs that require minimal or reduced physical labor. This includes any blue-collar jobs, waitressing, nursing, health care, hairdressing, retail, etc. Avoid anything that requires a lot of bending, stooping, or any manual work. Try to look for jobs that are from home or in an office setting.

Please avoid any type of work that requires physical exertion or severe over time until you feel better. Anything on the computer is good, answering phones, medical coding, affiliate marketing or freelance work. You can also opt to consider positions such as a social media specialist, copywriter, virtual assistant, data entry clerk, or graphic designer as these can be done from home. If you can't make changes or switch your career, ask your boss if you can make special accommodations. According to the American Disabilities Act, as an employer, you're always allowed to ask for that.

One of the reasons why fibromyalgia can be disabling is that there is a great deal of intensity when it comes to the pain. This puts added stress on the body, making it hard to perform tasks at work. Also, when fibromyalgia interferes with the brain, it can make you more forgetful.

If you feel that you need to apply for disability, then, by all means, do that. However, to qualify for disability you must prove that you have a severe impairment. You also need to prove that fibromyalgia limits your physical or mental ability to do work. Usually, you would have a physical examination and the doctor will ask you questions about how fibromyalgia impairs your work. It can be quite challenging to get SSDI or SSI, but it's worth a shot to try and open a case to apply.

Back in 2014, when I tried to apply, I researched law offices that dealt with cases like mine. I filled out a form and got a call back from the office to evaluate my case. Then I got in contact with a law office that could represent me. I received the forms in the mail and took it to my doctors and had them fill it out. The doctors were very descriptive on how fibromyalgia affected my working environment and my ability to carry out assigned duties in the job.

I then filled out various forms and kept their communication going back between my lawyer and myself. After seven months, I went in for a full physical and medical evaluation. It felt like a regular appointment at the doctor's office. They checked your vitals, blood pressure, everything. They had me stand up and move around just to see where the pain was.

I did not like the way I was treated there, as I had this title of "unable to work" attached to my chest. They had security guards right before the judge searching me and then leading me into the courtroom. The judge made me feel like it was my fault. I know she was just doing her job, but I felt so low at that point. I felt useless to society. Here I had all these career plans, and I had to accept my fate of not working.

I just want to let you know to not feel bad about yourself or blame yourself. You are not your condition, you are a whole person. Don't let anyone make you feel less than a human. I know it's hard to hear and to rise above it all. You are stronger than this and it will get better.

After waiting a few months, I got myself scheduled to go in front of the judge stating my case. I needed to prove that I was in so much pain that I could not work.

It was hard being heard in regards to my case and oftentimes I felt like my pain wasn't being taken seriously. It can be hard to prove that fibromyalgia affects performing everyday tasks.

The judge did ask me questions about fibro fog, what it is and how it affects my daily life. She wanted to know how it impaired me. I explained as accurately as possible. The lawyer who represented me was to my left side just listening and nodding. I told the judge how my concentration and cognitive function were affected due to having fibromyalgia. I discussed how it feels impossible to function every day and how this affects my work performance. I talked about the physical pain as well as my lowered energy levels. The judge listened attentively, and understood everything I said. My lawyer and I were actually under the impression that I was going to win my case. He turned to me and smiled, "I think we got this." Then he walked away.

Around two months later, I got the news that my case wasn't approved. They basically said even though I'm in discomfort, there are still jobs that I can do. I am *technically* not disabled. Plenty of cases with fibromyalgia have been approved, but mine wasn't. My guess is that they figured since it's still not an official medical condition according to them, then it wasn't going to be approved. I guess they thought I looked too healthy to be taken seriously. I couldn't even get partial SSDI or SSI. In order to be SSDI qualified, you needed at least 40 work credits, and I only had 17. According to the judge, I wasn't disabled enough to get SSI. I was only deemed as "uncomfortable" but not to where it would affect my work abilities. This was very false and upsetting news to hear. I wanted to appeal, but I knew that would take many months before I could go up in front of the judge again. I was at a loss for words feeling like I hit a huge bump or a fork in the road and did not know what to do.

After I received the news, I continued to study and get continuing education units to add onto my board certification. I did not work at all for two years and stayed with my family. In those two years, I focused on healing mentally and physically. I started seeing a therapist that dealt with chronic pain sufferers and in 2015, met with a wonderful woman who talked about how important it is to stay positive and to change my outlook on the situation.

I remember, though, when I first met my therapist, I explained to her the overwhelming emotions I was feeling as a result of my condition and the suffering it had caused me. I told her how I felt defeated, frustrated, helpless, depressed, and hopeless. I explained to her how my condition affected my social life, work, and how I needed way more rest than usual. I remember telling her how unfair I thought it was and how I got diagnosed at the worst time. I just kept asking her "why me"? She explained how changing my outlook would help. I did just that. I tried to accept that life's not fair and we all have something going on. In a way we all have something we suffer from. Some people have poor eyesight, some have visible physical disabilities, emotional and mental. It's about finding what works for you. It may take some time, but please try to work around your condition and don't ever give up.

The one thing I had to do in order for me to afford her was downgrade my insurance plan to HMO as opposed to PPO. HMO stands for health maintenance organization and PPO is preferred provider organization. With PPO you have the luxury of going to any specialist or doctor whereas HMO, you need a doctor to give you permission to see a specialist. The list of providers with HMO are also limited. I had to go on low-cost insurance on a sliding scale to afford her. I saw my therapist from the time of 2015-2018. It was a long process, but we worked out alternative options for working, even though it was only part-time. She helped me on the path that would make the most sense and how to deal with the emotional side of fibromyalgia. She had worked with patients in the past that have suffered lifelong chronic pain conditions. We went over lifestyle changes and new ways to look at difficult situations. Some of it was just about being as healthy as possible and practicing self-care. The changes my therapist and I suggested included light exercise and a gluten-free diet. According to her, gluten allergies can cause inflammation in the body and flare-ups. I tried it for a while, but personally found it hard to stick with. What I found to be great in terms of a diet is a plant-based diet as explained in my last chapter.

In about six months of therapy, my symptoms improved, but not completely, and I decided to think outside the box. One thing that I liked was to sell products on an online store. In 2016, I opened my first business where I sold handmade soap and other products in outlets such as online, Etsy, farmers markets and local boutiques. I was able to make handmade soap with the help of my family member and was able to sell them. It was actually very fun selling at farmers markets and interacting with the customers. I felt appreciated and people seemed to like my products. I had the business for five years. It was a great experience. Since 2016, my pain has gone away and is in complete remission. I will tell you more about how I got to this place in Chapters 7 and 8.

In 2017, I was able to keep my startup on the side and work in an office as an account manager. There was no physical strain and selling was actually interesting to me.

After my business closed in 2021, I had a second start-up, which was an online pet supply store. I was selling pet clothes, toys, and treats for cats and dogs. It was wonderful because there was minimal overhead and I did not have to keep any inventory. I drop-shipped all my items. That means that I did not have to worry about making trips to the UPS or post office because there was another middleman involved, I just had to worry about the marketing aspect, which was fun for me.

Finding usual jobs that did not fit the traditional mold worked for me. You might be feeling helpless and defeated trying to find something that works for you. All it takes is some planning and a determined spirit. Don't turn your nose up at any unique type of job.

What I did was focus on selling. I founded a product that I liked and knew a lot about. Then I decided to set up a blog and a website allowing product images to be uploaded with payment options. I ran all of this from my home and took payments online only. I found it to be exciting actually and very fulfilling. It was wonderful waking up and knowing I got sales or could make money online while I was sleeping.

I even did some affiliate marketing by setting up a website and having links to other companies' products. The nice thing about affiliate marketing is that there is no need to set up anything or upload product images. How it works is that when someone purchases from your website, you earn a great deal of commission from that sale. The sky's the limit with selling online.

Whatever you decide to do in terms of making money, keep an open mind. Here is something to consider. These are the must-haves and questions to ask yourself looking for a job when you have to fibromyalgia:

1. Is there flexi-time or ability to create your own hours?
2. Is there any physical labor involved?
3. Is there adequate medical leave or paid time off for doctor appointments?
4. Can the work be part-time?
5. Can you do it online?
6. Do you offer remote or telecommuting?

Just remember you are not a sufferer of fibromyalgia, you are a fibro warrior. You can find something out there that makes some money. It just takes a willful spirit and some time.

After I shut down my second start-up, I went on to volunteer for an animal rights organization and am currently writing. It's been a journey, but for the first time, I actually like what I'm doing.

Here are two things that I remember to help me. "Take everything one day at a time", and "seize new opportunities." Remember, where you start in life isn't always where you'll end up. Sometimes we envision ourselves in one career and it doesn't work out and instead we can actually receive something better. Always enjoy and have trust in the process. Sometimes finding the right fit for a job is trial and error. Take the plunge and see what works for you.

Chapter 5

Navigating the Emotional Rollercoaster of Fibromyalgia Diagnosis: Coping Strategies and Supportive Solutions

When you first received your diagnosis, you were probably shocked like I was. Maybe you were even relieved because you finally found out why you had been experiencing symptoms for so long. After being in pain for months not knowing what the cause is and then finally getting an answer, can stir up all types of emotions. You can feel peace, you can feel thankful that you have answers now. However, you probably don't want to hear the news that it's lifelong and that you'll be on medication for the rest of your life. Maybe, like me, you oppose medication and want to try a more natural solution. Remember, it's your body, don't make any rash decisions yet in your treatment plan. Always be gentle and kind to yourself and take your time. This is your decision to make on your mode of treatment. Try a bit of each treatment and give it a fair chance. See what works for you and what doesn't. Also, circumstances may have shifted right now in your life, but it's not the end of the world. You got this.

I want you to repeat to yourself that you are stronger than this. You will not be defined by fibromyalgia. Every day you practice self-care is one step closer to healing and relieving the pain. It does take time and you will feel a whole variety of emotions during this time, including anger, grief, depression, and even anxiety. You will grieve your old life before pain, but you don't have to let that emotion define you. Your life will change after fibromyalgia, but you will learn how to take care of yourself and check-in with your emotions. Your life may even end up in a different yet better direction. You can't predict the future, so don't give up and don't assume the worst.

I am not a licensed therapist, but the following activity helped me greatly. Now, I want you to try this exercise for me. Try to visualize for a moment what you're thinking of when dealing with your immediate emotion, whether it's anger, anxiety, etc. What is your automatic reaction? Then, as an exercise, try to draw that emotion. For example, if you're anxious, try to draw what it would look like if your anxiety were an object or a series of images. Make it as descriptive as possible. Use colored markers, pencils, and the like. Get creative and use your feelings to draw that image. If you're feeling sad, put it out there as an emotion. Unleash your inner artist and release that emotion into a personified thing on paper. I want you to practice this anytime you're feeling a negative emotion. Go back to the page where you drew that image and remember it. Now that you have done that, you'll always have a picture in your mind of what you're feeling instead of dealing with your emotions in a negative pattern. Instead of dwelling on the emotion, you can see it for what it is: simply an emotion. Sometimes when we feel bad, we take our emotions out in destructive ways. That is not good and can cause irreversible damage to you physically and mentally. This exercise will help with that and keep you feeling healthier and more positive.

Emotions Exercise

Emotions Exercise

Emotions Exercise

One feeling you will have, especially around your family or if you have children, is frustration. You might hear, "Mommy, why are you so tired?" or "I want you to take me to ballet class, not daddy." You have to explain to everyone why you feel the way you do and why you need help. Try explaining that to a five-year-old. It might be frustrating at first and hard for kids to understand, but there are ways to make it easier. My best advice is to have the whole family have a sit-down discussion and explain what both parents need to do to make things easier. Explain the diagnosis, the symptoms, and then address an action plan.

When you are around your friends you may feel too tired to go to every social event. They may feel let down, but most of all, you may feel terrible or too guilty to even face them and explain your symptoms. Ultimately, what you need more than anything is compassion from others and understanding. Maybe agree to an outing every two weeks for evening tea or the movies. Host a girl's night out close to you, or if you're a male, have a game night with your buddies. This way you won't feel sad or guilty like you're missing out or letting everyone down. Even though you have this condition, don't let your relationships suffer. You can have fun, be with others and still manage fibromyalgia. It's important to work around your symptoms and do things that you still find enjoyable. Just because you're in pain or discomfort doesn't mean you have to let go of your social life all together! You'll be pleasantly surprised when you realize how often your loved ones will be willing to try something new that might make you more comfortable.

It's important to not feel like your life has to be on hold until you feel better. Make as many adjustments as possible without sacrificing your normal. In fact, you might even end up creating a new normal that you like better! For instance, have a late-night meal with your spouse where the person that isn't in pain has to cook. Make shopping a team effort and then take turns doing the dishes and cleaning up. You could even order takeout food and make it a relaxing movie night where nobody has to cook or clean up! Do whatever feels best for you.

If you're living by yourself or with roommates, maybe do a fun night of taking turns cooking meals for each other. If you're by yourself, invite neighbors over for dinner or ask and see if maybe they want to bring food over and have a movie night.

Now if you're preparing meals by yourself, maybe take fewer trips to the grocery store and plan ahead. Come up with everything needed for a week or a week and a half, and then cook and have enough to store for leftovers. This takes away some of the labor time for preparing meals. If you have children, make enough food to store, and have prepared for school lunches, dinners etc. Also ask them to give you a helping hand and help around the house and participate in chores.

Here Are The Essential Do's and Don'ts for Recovering with Fibromyalgia

Do's:

1. Do include the entire family in helping out with your recovery.
2. Do write out your feelings in a journal.
3. Do practice the drawing exercises stated at the beginning of this chapter.
4. Do tell your spouse how you are feeling. Have a regular

check-in time with them.

5. Do work around your friends' schedules, but always try to carve out time with them.

Don'ts

1. Don't alienate or isolate yourself from people.
2. Don't do all the errands and chores by yourself.
3. Don't ignore time with your parents, relatives, etc. Keep them updated on how you feel. Don't feel embarrassed.
4. Don't keep symptoms to yourself, discuss everything with your doctor.
5. Avoid feeling overwhelmed by planning ahead.

Your job is to do what you can do to keep yourself healthy and together. Whether you're single or have a family. Everyone's situation is different. Find as much outside support as you can. If your job is to keep your family and household together, you do this as a team effort. If you're living at home by yourself, see if you can get groceries delivered from an ordering service and plan meals ahead of time to cut down cooking time. The more planned and active you are in participating in your treatment plan, the better it gets.

Try to have as many sit-down meetings with your loved ones as much as you can. If you can't meet-up in person, have as many virtual meetups as you can. Get creative when it comes to connecting with others. For example, host a virtual event and have a party with friends with music playing in the background. Or do a virtual fibromyalgia meet-up group and have a fun ice breaker question and Q&A. Start to make everything enjoyable again.

I will be certain that during your path to recover, you'll likely feel an array of overwhelming emotions. At first, you might be in an emotional state of disbelief when you're still processing the diagnosis. Then, you may reach a point of acceptance. Some reach a point of sadness. Life has changed, but *has* it?

You're still the same person inside and everyone still loves you. Now is the time to reach out to those closest to you and your community. Say yes to those community events. Go to potluck dinners, make new friends or even join an in-person fibromyalgia chronic pain support group. You'll meet dozens of people in the same boat as you and you can build some wonderful friendships from there. Help each other out by scheduling outings and talking about your experience with others who will likely relate to you. This isn't the end all be all. Things may have changed, but it isn't a death sentence or the end. You will handle this better with time.

Chapter 6

The Crucial Role of Your Support Network for Managing Fibromyalgia

Your family and friends are imperative to your well-being and can offer support during times of suffering from fibromyalgia. Without them, it will make your healing process very hard. It's important to have your social support circle developed. There are many places where you can also meet people to reach out for help. Ask relatives, your immediate family, your significant other, friends, support groups and local community centers.

There are many ways you can share the news with others. It's important to pick the right time to tell your loved ones: When it comes to sharing the devastating diagnosis, it's important to be calm and be in a neutral environment. The best way is to break it gently and try to avoid high emotions when talking about how you found out about your diagnosis. It's a good idea to be as relaxed as possible to avoid any upset.

Make sure to sit everyone down together in a room and get them comfortable. This is so there is less chance of an unexpected reaction. Then, the best way to break the news is to kindly discuss your diagnosis and treatment plan. Talk about the symptoms, your level of discomfort and how it will impact you. Also, explain everything that the doctor talked about and your plan on how to get better. Let them know your participation in recovering. Do get everyone's input and explain how you will need their help. Let them know the importance of them having you there to help you in your recovery. Maybe even have an open discussion on ways they can get involved. Listen to their feedback and answer any questions that they may have on fibromyalgia. Talk about things such as treatment plans, recovery time, what fibromyalgia exactly is. Make it easy for them to understand and their role in helping you feel better.

Let your loved ones take in all the information and process it to see what they say and their given response. Whether or not they take it well is not your fault or something you should even have to worry about. Don't take it personally. You also are in recovery and you need to also accept responsibility for taking active participation in healing. Do let them know that you will need help around the house and also in receiving support from them. If you already know what specific type of support you'll need, tell them.

If your spouse has questions, now is the time to answer. Do offer them to go with you to doctors appointments, therapy, and the like, if that's something you're comfortable with. You will need help from these specialists. It might take your significant other a while to adjust to the new situation, but you need them there by your side.

If you happen to be the caretaker of someone with fibromyalgia, then scheduling time to relax with them, and have a fun outing time is important. Do keep some type of scheduled time with them and always offer open communication. Maybe offer them a ride to the doctor's office appointment. Any small gesture helps. Let them know that you care.

Let's say you live by yourself and are having a hard time coming up with a support group. The best thing to do is join a pain relief support group. The best would be one that caters to fibromyalgia, but any pain support group would work. Sometimes they will have one strictly for arthritis sufferers, but they do welcome all types of pain-inflicted individuals.

If you're with a partner, or married, try to have them alternate tasks with you. One day you take out the garbage, the next day he/she does. Take turns with the household chores and cooking. Also, don't forget to schedule date nights and fun nights out to get your mind off the condition that you have. You are not your fibromyalgia, so have fun, relax and enjoy yourself.

Right now I want you to think off the top of your head a list of five people you could reach out to. You'll be surprised when you try this that you will have others to connect with. Try to see who has time to get together, maybe share a meal with a bunch of friends, and have a night together playing board games. Not every activity you plan has to be anything too physical.

Another thing you can do is find a workout buddy. Maybe try someone in your fibromyalgia support group that has similar workout goals. Get together three days a week for a brisk walk around the neighborhood. Try taking classes with them at your local gym in something low-impact like Pilates. Do anything you can that allows you to have relationships with others while improving your health.

If you have kids, go to a local community program that has activities designed for families so everyone can participate. This could be like a group camping trip or maybe a day at the aquarium. The more you're able to participate in life, the better you will feel. Remember, please allow yourself enough time to rest up though as needed.

Another thing that would really help is to buy a planner and ahead of time schedule days of when you plan your activities or perhaps maybe need to run errands. That way you'll be prepared ahead of time and know when to rest, how to plan out your day, and you'll be able to make enough time for self-care.

Always have "me" time. Schedule a day at a spa, or read a book outdoors while sipping green tea. Give yourself a break and celebrate small wins. Take it slowly in your self-care program and build from there. Start small with your socializing and activities and then when you have more energy, build up to a full social life. Don't be afraid to reach out to your friends, family members, and support groups. Embark on new friendships, and keep in touch with old ones. People will want to help you and be there for you, but it takes courage to open up about your condition and how it impacts your life. No one should treat you differently from it or make you feel bad. If they do, maybe re-evaluate your relationship and give it time. They will come around.

It's so important to have your social network there for you to provide emotional support. Get to know people in your position. You won't feel so alone and you'll begin to feel a new normal again.

Reach out to your extended family and relatives and see if they can provide some assistance and support. Don't ignore holiday gatherings or opportunities to see them. When you're dealing with an illness, it's best to stay in contact with all of your loved ones including immediate and extended family members.

The more support you have, the better you will feel. You will even meet some new friends along the way while in treatment.

You have to also be your own best friend and be kind and good to yourself. Self-love despite your illness is so important. Don't let this damage your self-esteem. Use this moment as a growing process to use the tools I gave you and treatment methods. Also, be nice to yourself and engage in new hobbies or watch funny movies. Everything works to cheer you up.

Here are some fun activities to do during your own time:

1. Make something using creativity just for fun.
2. Try a new recipe and cook a new dish.
3. Get a manicure and pedicure.
4. Go to a spa and get a facial treatment.
5. Go to the hair salon and have your hair done.
6. Buy new makeup at the department store counter and have someone do your makeup.
7. Indulge in chocolate or your favorite dessert.
8. Go shopping for new clothes.
9. Go to the farmers market and shop for new groceries.
10. Spend the day at the movies and treat yourself to popcorn.

As you can see there are many activities and fun things you can do in your spare time and to pamper yourself as well. Feel free to come up with your own ideas.

Try to schedule one day a week even just for a few hours, where you can spend quality time by yourself and treat yourself. It could even be something as simple as watching your favorite tv show or movie. Maybe do a playlist of relaxing music and listen to that for half an hour. You need your time to unwind, even if it's for a short period. If you are having mobility issues, maybe have someone drive you somewhere, let's say to a park and spend your day soaking in the outside sunshine.

You may find out that with more free time, you can relax and take care of yourself. You may have to make adjustments in your life, but with emotional support from others, you can feel more at ease when doing this. Broaden your circle of friends and get to know others in similar situations. Ask them questions about their hobbies or how they are finding time to take care of themselves. Go as a group and take a yoga class. You will have so much fun trying to get better if you go as a group. You don't have to feel alone in all of this. You'll be amazed at what people want to help you with. I found a lot of support in my religious community and support groups.

Keep being open with your immediate family on ways they can help and they will be there for you. You need to understand how important it is to have people in your life that are on your side. If anyone tries to make you feel bad or like a burden then focus on others that do care and want to help. You will get better in time, but you can't do it alone. Reach out, don't be afraid to be open and ask for help.

Chapter 7

Maximizing Collaborative Care: Strategies for Effective Partnership with Your Doctor and Specialists

When you get your first official diagnosis, it's crucial to ensemble a team of doctors and specialists that can communicate with you and work with you on your treatment plan. There are several people you need on your team to recover. One is a doctor who is your primary care physician. If you can't afford one, please look into the Affordable Care Act so that you can get insurance. There are many great doctors that accept this insurance. Also, if you are working, see if you can get access to discounts for complementary treatments as well as this can be useful for you. Certain insurance companies provide coverage for services like acupuncture, chiropractic care, and holistic medicine. I feel that each specialty has value and should be at least tried out. I personally have had great results with herbs and massage therapy. In addition, I also worked with a naturopath that recommended the right supplements and vitamins that helped me. These included fish oil and folic acid. The fish oil I used helped with inflammation and pain. Folic acid lowered my homocysteine levels which can improve the MTHFR gene expression that can cause fibromyalgia.

One thing that's important is to work with the right type of doctor. Your primary care physician should give you a referral to a rheumatologist for treating fibromyalgia. Rheumatologists specialize in this type of care. They are highly trained doctors that deal with inflammatory diseases. They work on issues surrounding tissues, joints, etc. They can go over different types of options for you to treat your condition. A rheumatologist can help discuss medication or devise another type of plan. They can also teach you how to properly bend, move the body and increase mobility. What a rheumatologist helped me with was certain recovery methods such as the correct way to move that helped. They can also help you find alternative treatment and holistic methods as well and can support you in your recovery.

There are some things to make note of. First off, in the beginning, it takes a bit of time and effort to find the right doctor. Do your research. It's important to schedule appointments with multiple doctors and take note of those who actively listen to your concerns and needs. Ideally, you want to find a physician who is not only knowledgeable but also compassionate. Look for a doctor with whom you feel comfortable discussing your health. Look for someone who genuinely cares about your well-being and with whom you have a good rapport. To do this, ask yourself the questions below and keep track of your answers for each regarding each doctor:

1. Have they worked with fibromyalgia patients?
2. Are they open to finding other alternatives than just the standard mode of medication?
3. Are they kind, compassionate, and caring (by validating you when you discuss your symptoms)?
4. Do they have a good list of specialists to recommend for you? Do they give referrals?

5. Do they make you feel ike a person and not just another number?

When you do see a doctor, be sure to also make note of the treatment options available for you. During your initial visit, you and the doctor will likely go over your medical history and fibromyalgia symptoms. Once diagnosed, you can see if there are tests that can be run to uncover the root cause of your fibromyalgia.

These might include food allergy tests to see if you're gluten intolerant or the tissue transglutaminase antibody (tTG) IgA class test that looks for celiac disease. These tests can also simply rule out any sensitivities. Normally, a dietician or nutritionist would run these tests. To see a specialist in this matter, you would still need a referral. I would say a dietician would know more about the specific food allergy tests but either or would suffice.

If you can, I highly recommend getting a referral to a dietician that is in network and have them work on a meal plan. It's important to see a specialist about your diet so that you can find a meal plan that alleviates your symptoms and makes you feel your best. During your first appointment with the dietician, they will assess your current diet, give you a lifestyle change protocol. They will ask about your symptoms and maybe run tests and then from here see what changes can be made. This is crucial for fibromyalgia sufferers because diet is very important and any food sensitivities you do have, must be looked into.

Another thing to consider is working with a naturopath. They can help with trying out supplements and herbs that soothe fibromyalgia symptoms. A lot of naturopaths take insurance, so check it out and see who's in network.

A chiropractor is another also great practitioner as they can help realign the spine. They also help with a great deal of pain related issues including fibromyalgia, so be sure to consider seeing one.

Try to work with as many people as you can and stick to the same practitioners and specialists so that they can help you with your individual needs and get to know those needs on a deeper level as time goes on. If you jump around too much, you might not get the best, personalized treatment plan for you. When finding the right care and trying to put together the right team, take it step by step and prioritize finding those who are knowledgeable and passionate.

Alternative Fibromyalgia Treatments Worth Exploring

Alternative Medicine –

Finding an acupuncturist or massage therapist to get ongoing treatment from is a great idea when it comes to alleviating your symptoms. It's best to see if you can get a referral from your primary care doctor. Then, once you find an acupuncturist or massage therapist that you like, develop a relationship with them, you will likely be seeing them for a long time to come.

If you can't get a referral from your primary care doctor, you can purchase low-cost supplemental insurance that provides discount plans for both specialists. Keep in mind that a high price for a service does not necessarily yield better results.

Personal Training –

Now onto your fitness. Working with a personal trainer is a great way to discuss fitness goals and create an exercise regimen that alleviates your fibromyalgia pain. You can start out with something non-committal like five sessions and then use the practice exercises that you learned during training. Depending on your goals, it's probably best to find a trainer that deals with chronic pain and how to work around it. Some personal trainers also help with diets and meal plans, so finding this might help you combine the personal trainer and dietician roles into one!

Group Workout Classes –

If you feel comfortable, try attending group classes at a gym that offer low-impact exercises. There are many low-cost gym memberships or discounted classes that could help if you're tight on money. This is a great way to get in your low-impact workouts without having to pay for a personal trainer. It might also allow you to feel like part of the community.

1-on-1 Therapy -

Lastly, if you need help emotionally dealing with your condition, I would recommend a therapist. They can offer different types of counseling for pain management and helpful ways to work around your condition. There are many types of therapy out there including cognitive behavioral therapy, dialectical behavioral therapy and talk therapy that can help. Cognitive therapy can help you sort out your thoughts and provide you with a new way of thinking. It can banish negative thinking patterns and help you cope more easily with your condition. I personally used dialectical behavioral therapy because it taught me the importance of mindfulness and radical acceptance. This is when you accept something and not try to change it. It's a very self-soothing technique. Mindfulness breathing exercises like focusing on a single moment can reduce my painful symptoms by redirecting my focus on something else.

It's important to keep a list of your team in a notebook and change things up if you're not feeling completely supported by those on your team. Any time you do an intake with a first appointment, be honest and upfront on who you're currently working with. Have a list of specialists you're currently seeing and ask questions. Be very honest and try to gather as much helpful information as possible. This will help keep you organized and on top of your treatment plan.

Chapter 8

Navigating the Road to Fibromyalgia Recovery: Tips for a Smoother Journey

Recovery is a process and sometimes it's a long one, so be patient. However, I'm here to share with you some of the methods that have worked for me so that you can have a smoother recovery. I'm just sharing my personal experience, so feel free to pick and choose and experiment with different ideas to see what works best for you. To get the most out of your treatment plan, I would say mix it up as much as you can but stay consistent on healing yourself every day. That way, you'll always have the end goal in mind but you'll be able to optimize your healing as you go because you'll continually find better solutions that work for you.

One of the first things that helped with my aches and the burning feeling was CBD oil and cream. CBD is known as Cannabidoil, and in a cream form, it can help reduce pain. It has been known to provide relief for common ailments such as arthritis, muscle aches and much more. I've given CBD to one of my family members and they reported a reduction in their arthritis pain. You can usually purchase CBD from a health food store or online.

I have used CBD on all my tender points and it really works for me. It provides a numbing feeling on the muscles and greatly reduces any pain. Make sure to ask if it has THC which stands for tetrahydrocannabinol in it. That's the stuff that gets you high. Most CBD products take it out, but you want to be sure and be safe. THC is what gives CBD the psychoactive effects and we don't want that.

The one thing I love about CBD is that it really has a cooling and calming effect on the muscles. It slightly dulls the pain and then relaxes you. If you want the full benefit, I would recommend mixing CBD with lavender oil for a relaxing and aromatherapeutic experience. This may not work for you, but this is from my own personal experience with different pain-relieving creams and I felt that CBD worked the best. Some creams already come with a scent. Some of my favorite scents for CBD cream are peppermint, lavender, and lemon verbena.

Another thing to try is essential oils, which you can put in a diffuser or apply directly onto the skin. These essential oils may help with fibromyalgia pain as a direct form of treatment but must be diluted with a carrier oil when applied directly to the skin. Popular carrier oils include almond or apricot oil. Caution: essential oils should not be swallowed. If you put it in a diffuser, it acts as aromatherapy and can be used to open up the lung airways or provide a relaxing effect on the body and the nervous system. The best oils that I tried to help my fibromyalgia pain are eucalyptus, peppermint and lavender oil. My favorite out of all of them is lavender. This is because it relaxes you and also puts you at ease making your whole body less inclined to feel pain. Once again, experiment and see what you like. Also, be diligent about it. Once I got into the routine of consistently using lavender oil, it helped. I applied twice a day to the sore spots.

I am on the fence about acupuncture, but for some people

with fibromyalgia, it works. Certain parts of the body respond to this and going to repeat treatments can help. It is known to reduce inflammation and the small needles placed in stimulating the release of your body's own pain killer, which is endorphins. They also are known to take part in calming your brain. However, this can get quite expensive, so that's something to consider before trying it out.

Massage therapy is another option. Try to see if you can get a discount or a package deal on Groupon as it cuts down the cost. Some great ones to try are Swedish massage and deep tissue massage. Ask your massage therapist to apply light pressure in the beginning and then go from there.

Herbs are great and they really helped me deal with my pain and fatigue. Some of the herbs that help fight fibromyalgia include echinacea, black cohosh, cayenne, lavender, milk thistle, and B vitamins. I really like B vitamins because they help with my energy levels. Milk thistle is also great for balancing hormones. Hormonal imbalances are one contributing factor for developing fibromyalgia. I personally did not have much luck with cayenne, but it can help for others. What it does is block substance P, which is a pain receptor. When it's blocked, you won't experience a pain signal to the brain therefore dulling the aches. One caveat, please make sure not to take cayenne pepper pills on an empty stomach and build up your tolerance to it.

Just remember to always consult with your doctor before you try anything.

The other thing that helped a lot is to buy a notebook and keep a diary. Track your symptoms and healing modalities and record how you feel. Take note of your pain, moods and how you respond to treatment overall. Start with a schedule and make note of your day and include all the time you have for self-care. Make sure to carve out time for each day in taking care of your condition. This is especially important if you're just starting out and experimenting with different healing methods! Keeping track of what works and what doesn't will help you optimize your recovery as time goes on.

Now onto a very important part of recovery: movement. At first you may feel like any form of exercise is too painful and daunting. I totally understand the feeling. I assure you that it will get better, but you have to build up gradually. One thing that can help is getting some light brisk walking in. If you can only do 10 minutes a day that's fine. Remember, progress is progress. I know as I have been there.

I know exactly what it's like to want to stay in bed all day and to also feel the emotional side of fibromyalgia. I know that it's hard to take that first step. It's kind of like learning a new language or skill as it takes time and practice. When you are in chronic pain, the last thing on your mind is moving your body. However, once you start moving, you will feel a lot better. Just make sure that you give yourself enough rest between workouts. I would aim for working out five days a week and have two full-day rest periods. These workouts will help beat chronic fatigue, which is associated with fibromyalgia.

Some workouts that work well include Pilates. Pilates is a form of exercise that is not just for dancers. It was founded by physical trainer Joseph Pilates and initially aimed at dancers but anyone can benefit from this workout. It combines strength-building and toning. The major emphasis is building your core and using that to stabilize your body. As a result, muscles are elongated and you get that sleek leaner look.

Anything involving the water provides healing to the joints. This includes water aerobics or swimming laps. Swimming is a great way to get your toning and cardio in at the same time. It does not add stress to the joints and instead provides support. You can even take a dip in the jacuzzi afterward for a soothing effect on the muscles. I also want to mention that water aerobics is also great because you can use light foam weights in the water and can get cardio in at the same time. Many fitness centers offer water aerobics as a class.

Cycling is great as it improves cardiovascular fitness as well as provides joints with support and increased flexibility. It can prevent a wide variety of health issues such as heart disease. For usage make sure you consider getting bottoms with padding in the butt to make the bike seat feel more comfortable. For women, use a sturdy sports bra, especially if you're on the busty end.

Yoga is great as well for flexibility, mind and body. It allows you to become aware of your breathing and increases body awareness. It allows you to connect with yourself. Over time, you will be stronger and more flexible. Your muscles will tone and you will feel better overall. One of my favorite forms of yoga that I did included Ashtanga yoga. I felt that it really worked in terms of stretching my muscles and strengthening them. This is because this form of yoga focuses on muscle training and develops physical strength as a result, you will feel stronger physically and throughout the body. With consistent practice of yoga, you will be able to start improving joint health and be able to participate more in daily tasks. It is also great for your mind and relaxes you as well.

Tai chi is also a great form of martial arts that makes you feel powerful mentally and physically. It's great for fibromyalgia and can be a wonderful form of recovery for PTSD. It provides great physical and mental benefits. The inner healing you get from tai chi can really help you recover from trauma. The movements are slow and gentle and the breathing is controlled. This allows for focus on muscle strength and flexibility, It can help reduce pain sores in people with fibromyalgia. Sometimes, I would do tai chi and alternate the workout with Pilates as well.

Now, what I did to stay on top of everything was keep a workout record and blocked out time for exercise. I tracked this on a notepad. I would set a schedule and goal such as working out five days a week for twenty minutes. Then, I would build up to cardio five days a week for 30 minutes with two days of strength. The cardio would be either light walking or cycling, and then use Pilates to build strength. You can also use resistance bands as well as they help, or your own body weight. The main focus on cardio is low-impact workouts followed by strength training exercises. Remember, go at your own pace. If you just want to focus on 10 minutes of walking or stretching a day, then that's completely fine. The main key is to stay consistent and keep the end goal in mind: healing.

Also, don't forget to stretch. This is important to prevent injury and remain flexible. Please stretch before and after a workout. Stretching will also improve your range of motion. A few stretches to do that worked for me include; shoulder rolls, side bends, calf stretches, downward facing dog and side arm stretches to name a few. One thing I did after a cool down stretch was use a heating pad or bathe in Epsom salts to soothe the muscle. I liked combining Epsom salt with Himalayan salt to soothe and heal the body.

A lot of people suffering from fibromyalgia gain weight, so these exercises can help prevent that and maintain good health. Make sure to track your progress in your daily log or journal. Start small and build up. Soon you will be able to work out more and more. Don't be afraid to push yourself, but don't overdo it. Listen to your body. It's better to build up slowly than to go super explosive on your workouts and then get injured.

Another thing that I liked after a workout was using TENS, which reduces the intensity of pain in adults with fibromyalgia and also acts as a form of rehabilitation. TENS stands for transcutaneous electrical nerve stimulation. It can be purchased in a wide variety of stores including local drug stores. I purchased mine from Tenspro. What TENS does and how it works is that it sends electrodes and pulses to the area of where the pain is. What you do is that you stick the electrodes around where you've got pain, and the device sends a little electricity throughout the area. This reduces pain and stiffness by decreasing pain perception. It activates nerve pathways via mild electrical currents, to reduce the pain being felt.

These methods will help reduce pain and fatigue associated with fibromyalgia. Remember to take supplements, a fish oil and vitamin D supplement would be good. Fish oil provides the brain with Omega 3 which improves brain function and can reduce inflammation in the body. Vitamin D helps with depression and moods. Get outside and get enough sunshine, and keep being socially active. Eat a balanced diet with lots of fruits and vegetables and workout consistently. Drink green tea in the morning, water and kombucha tea. Kombucha tea is a form of fermented tea that can be served warm or chilled that helps with energy levels. I just know that you will see a great improvement in the way you feel.

Another key factor in healing is also tending to your spiritual needs. It's very important to stay connected to some type of community that involves prayer or any type of spiritual healing. It's important to remain social and stay connected with others. We are our bodies, minds and spirits and it's a good idea to ask for help from a higher being. This will also help gain perspective on those moments when you are suffering and who to turn to for support.

Always keep in touch with your whole support team because getting better requires a team effort. This means your primary care physician, family, friends, specialists, and anyone else helping you out. You will get better, it just takes time and effort.

Lastly, here is a journal for you to fill out. In it, write about what treatment methods were your favorite, what worked for you and what didn't. Always make sure to have time to practice self-care. Make use of your schedule, stick to it and in the notes section, reflect on what you felt was the most effective for you. Ask yourself each week, how do you feel now? What has been working so far? It helps to check on your progress from time to time. This will give you a better idea of what to stick to in your treatment plan. Remember, mix and match these above methods explained in the beginning of this chapter. Feel free to experiment or even add your own treatment methods. All of this does help and pay off in the end with the desired outcome of feeling better.

Progress Report and Reflection

SUNDAY

Morning:

Afternoon:

Evening:

Other Notes:

MONDAY

Morning:

Afternoon:

Evening:

Other Notes:

TUESDAY

Morning: ______________________________

Afternoon: ______________________________

Evening: ______________________________

Other Notes: ______________________________

WEDNESDAY

Morning:

Afternoon:

Evening:

Other Notes:

THURSDAY

Morning:

Afternoon:

Evening:

Other Notes:

FRIDAY

Morning:

Afternoon:

Evening:

Other Notes:

SATURDAY

Morning:

Afternoon:

Evening:

Other Notes:

General Notes:

Chapter 9

How a Plant-based Diet Can Heal Fibromyalgia

Many holistic practitioners believe that a plant-based or vegan diet can help heal symptoms of fibromyalgia. This is because a plant-based diet produces an anti-inflammatory effect on the body, which is exactly what fibromyalgia patients need. When inflammation is down, you're less likely to feel pain in your muscles from fibromyalgia. Think of anti-inflammatory foods as cooling down a burning sensation or putting out a fire. I know for me, the fibromyalgia pain went away gradually and overtime it became obsolete. I know my diet helped with this.

Another thing is that a plant-based diet can also increase your energy levels. Now, in the beginning of your recovery process, you may have had trouble getting all of your movement and activity levels up. This is why diet is that much more important to alleviate your symptoms of fibromyalgia: a plant-based diet can increase your energy, reduce your pain, and alleviate cognitive difficulties. All of these benefits will make it easier for you to increase your activity levels, get in a healthy amount of movement, and speed up your healing journey.

The plant-based diet has never been more popular, and for good reason. According to the National Academy of Sports Medicine (NASM, 2022), there has been a steady increase in plant-based diets such as veganism and vegetarianism over the last several decades. This is primarily because the studies show that plant-based diets reduce the risk of cardiovascular disease. Studies have also shown that plant-based diets help to prevent a wide variety of conditions due to the decrease in fat that's found in animal products.

Plant-based diets rely primarily, or entirely, on plant-based foods. Don't worry, if you're not ready to go fully vegan yet, there are several subtypes of diets that fall under the domain of plant-based diets. These include vegan, vegetarian, pescatarian, lacto-ovo-vegetarian, or flexitarian diets. We'll go into actionable ways that you can modify your diet later on in this chapter.

One reason that plant-based diets are gaining popularity is because they reduce the risk of obesity. When you're overweight, it can only make fibromyalgia symptoms worse and cause added stress to the body. Obesity is also a major risk factor for heart disease and diabetes, and individuals who follow a plant-based diet, especially vegan diets, consume fewer calories and tend to carry a lower BMI than those who follow omnivorous diets (NASM, 2022). As you can see, finding plant-based sources of nutrition provides you with fewer calories and saturated fat. This in turn creates a lower BMI (Body Mass Index). Less obesity risk means less chronic pain and added stress to the joints.

Remember when I mentioned in Chapter 2 about the link between slow oxidizers and fibromyalgia? Well, sufferers of slow oxidizers respond well to being a vegetarian or pescatarian. They can also eat moderate amounts of fish which would be very helpful for joint inflammation. Salmon is a great source as it acts as an anti-inflammatory. If you're vegan, there are some great protein alternatives. Slow oxidizers can also eat more grains than fast oxidizers. Some of the personality traits of slow oxidizers are that they are often laid back and easy going, but may suffer from lack of energy or depression. Now, what do I mean by grains? I mean mostly millet, quinoa, whole grains, all types of rice and cornmeal, basically complex carbs not simple carbs.

As you can see, a plant-based diet can improve your overall health in addition to reducing pain associated with fibromyalgia. A plant-based diet can greatly increase your quality of life, quality of sleep, and general health status. Your health and pain levels go hand in hand with each other. The healthier you are, the less pain you have. The main ways to get healthier are through rest, diet, vitamins, and exercise.

- *Unveiling the Truths Behind Plant-Based Diets: Dispelling 3 Common Myths*

Now, you may have heard the negatives about plant-based diets. Well, I'm here to dispel the myths so that you feel free to experiment with what works best for you. These are the myths about plant-based diets according to NASM:

MYTH #1 - Many plant-based diets are high in soy and phytoestrogens, which may have negative health effects due to their potential hormone-disrupting capacities.

Here's the thing. Plant-based diets do have some soy, but not enough to count as a risk factor in many hormonal conditions. True risks associated with soy and phytoestrogens derived from food are relatively small, and, in some cases, they may provide risk reduction for some diseases and minor risk increases for others. In one example, soy intake is associated with a reduced risk of breast cancer in women (NASM, 2022).

MYTH #2 - There are inadequate protein sources in plant-based diets.

When it comes to not being able to get enough protein in a plant-based diet, that is entirely false. I will tell you the sources of protein that you can have with a plant-based basic vegan diet, and even include a shopping guide at the end of his chapter for you to follow. It's very doable and can provide a balanced diet providing enough nutrients and protein. You have nothing to worry about on this vegan diet and it can lower the risk of pain and many other illnesses. When you have fibromyalgia, pain is felt throughout the body, so a plant-based diet can be just what you need.

MYTH #3 - There are inadequate vitamins and nutrients in plant-based diets.

In regards to nutrient deficiencies, well, in any diet you will gain some more nutrients than others, but you can easily take a multivitamin to help balance out whatever you might be missing. With a regular non-plant-based diet, you'll be getting less iron. However, plant-based diets are often lower in calcium; but, they are also often much higher in vitamin C, folate, fiber, and vitamin E. My pescatarian diet has been recorded to have the highest long-chain omega-3 fatty acid intake and the highest vitamin D intake. However, I do take a multivitamin every day to make sure my body functions properly.

❖ *Fibro-Friendly Food Finds: A Plant-Based Shopping Guide*

There are many ways to switch over to a plant-based diet in a manageable, simple way. If you like the taste of meat, start with meatless products such as:

Plant-based sausages
Plant-based hot dogs
Plant-based chicken
Plant-based ground meat

Make sure to consume lots of legumes, whole grains, fruits and vegetables. Meanwhile, your tastebuds will grow accustomed to your new diet and you won't even miss the taste of animal-based products. Overtime as a result, your health will improve and your fibromyalgia symptoms will be minimized.

Eating a wide variety of fruits and vegetables will calm down inflammation and make the fibromyalgia pain less and less. If you slip up, don't worry, just go back on the right track. It doesn't have to be perfect, but everyday you should be doing something for your condition to recover faster.

If you're pescatarian, just add or include eggs, dairy and seafood. One thing to remember is to avoid sugar and highly processed foods. This includes white bread, desserts, candy, crackers, etc. You may drink wine in moderation. Remember to eat lots of vegetables, fruits and whole grains. Avoid soda and fruit juices, but drink lots of water and tea. I personally prefer green tea for energy and healing.

I personally am a pescatarian, because I feel like my inflammation is down and moods are better when I'm having lots of high fatty fish. This includes seafood such as wild caught salmon, tuna, mackerel, and herring. Personally, I've always loved meat, chicken, turkey and fish. I just always had those as staple items in my diet ever since I was a kid. When I decided to go fully vegan, it was more for ethical reasons. I had a hard time without my salmon, though, so I decided not to part ways with it and find a happy medium. I became a pescatarian. You're allowed to have fish, eggs and milk on this diet, but I personally don't like dairy because it tends to bother my stomach and still causes inflammation in my body. Remember that you can always cater your diet in this way toward whatever works best for healing your fibromyalgia symptoms. This shopping guide is designed to be modified toward what works best for you! To begin is a list of plant-based protein sources that you can find at your local grocery store.

Plant-Based Protein Sources To Include In Your Grocery List:

Tofu
Tempeh
Seitan
Beans
Lentils
Nutritional yeast
Spelt
Chia seed
Edamame

Spirulina

Peanuts

Green peas

Soy

Pumpkin seed

Almonds

Soy milk

Seeds

Spinach

Oats

Broccoli

Types of Carbohydrates To Consume

Quinoa

Amaranth

Gluten-free bread, pasta

Sourdough Bread

Oatmeal

Cornmeal

Buckwheat

Brown Rice

Wild Rice

Sweet Potato

Potato

Fruits To Consume:

Pineapple

Guava

Strawberries
Kiwi
Dried Fruits
Banana
Avocado
Apples
Pears
Peaches
Nectarines
Grapes
Blueberries
Raspberries

Vegetables To Consume:

Squash
Leeks
Cucumber
Tomatoes
Zucchini
Broccoli
Leafy Greens
Spinach
Carrots
Red bell peppers
Peas
Beets

❖ *From My Kitchen to Yours: A Step-by-Step Guide to Crafting My 2 Favorite Plant-Based Recipes*

One of my favorite dishes is Tofu Pad Thai. You won't miss any meat products and it tastes amazing. Tofu is somewhat squishy in consistency, but it's delicious and can be served in so many ways. Another thing I like to cook is tempeh, which is generally cooked in boiling water and steamed usually till it's a soft, but firm consistency. The taste is somewhat nutty, but one thing I like to do is cut the tempeh after it has been cooked into small cubes. Then sauté it with vegetables, noodles and a spicy Thai peanut sauce. It is so good and flavorful.

A lot of plant-based meat brands use pea protein, but it's done mixed with other ingredients to give a meat-like consistency. It's usually flavored with hickory or Worchester sauce for a smokey flavor. When prepared, either in a frying or sauce pan, it looks like actual meat is cooking.

Another one of my favorite things to make is vegan tacos. For this, you would use a frying pan to cook the plant-based meat, or whatever you decide to use for the base, until it's just like regular meat. The trick is to use medium heat when cooking so it develops into a meaty texture. First in a small bowl, blend the seasonings together with the plant-based meat and use a fork until evenly distributed. Use a wooden spoon and stir till it achieves the right consistency. Cook in the frying pan or saucepan, but don't overcook it. The plant-based meat will start to look like regular meat. For more protein and variety, add black beans to it. Then garnish with avocados, cilantro, tomatoes, lettuce, non-dairy cheese and anything else you want to add.

As of now, I have been symptom free since 2016. I have not had any flare ups and I don't take medicine for fibromyalgia. I do take fish oil, vitamind3, a multiple vitamin, and B12 vitamins for energy. I can concentrate better and keep up with daily tasks. I can work out six days a week for 40 minutes without any pain. I can move more freely and I can keep up with my niece and nephews' high energy. I sleep about 8-9 hours a night, sometimes a 30-minute nap in the afternoon.

You too will recover in time, and you may have some setbacks along the way. Do not lose hope. You don't have to have pain for the rest of your life. You can have a full and fulfilling life with fibromyalgia. You can work and have friends, relationships, family, and hobbies. You have to stay positive and believe that you can recover. Don't be timid and don't be afraid to reach out to others for support. Remember to build a good team of doctors and care specialists. Take care of yourself and in no time you will feel better. You may feel frustrated like it will never get better, but it's a temporary feeling and it's not based on truth. I know that you can recover and get closer to better health.

I hope this book helped you out and the information is a helpful tool for you to think about and steps to take in the recovery process. It's not the end of the world that you have fibromyalgia, you just need to adjust things. I call all my fibromyalgia sufferers and friends "fibro lights" because they have a light that shines and beams inside of them. You now have a light of healing inside your body for recovery. Be well and stay positive.

References

ARLTMA. (n.d.). Fibromyalgia. Retrieved from https://arltma.com/newsletters/fibromyalgia/

Deep Dive into The Plant-Based Diet. National Academy of Sports Medicine. (2022). Retrieved from https://www.nasm.org/

Printed in the USA
CPSIA information can be obtained
at www.ICGtesting.com
LVHW060845080823
754340LV00017B/1043

9 781734 519860